Without Animals Life Is Not Worth Living

CW01426106

Also by Freya Mathews and published by Ginninderra Press
Journey to the Source of the Merri

Freya Mathews

Without Animals
Life Is Not Worth Living

G
P

Acknowledgements

This essay first appeared in *Between the Species* 7, 2007.

Without Animals Life Is Not Worth Living
ISBN 978 1 76041 092 6
Copyright © text Freya Mathews 2016
Cover image from *The Book of Hours of Joanna the Mad*, Bruges,
1486–1506, British Library Add.18852, fol. 412 R
Artwork on page 55 by Rainer Mathews

First published in this form 2016 by
GINNINDERRA PRESS
PO Box 3461 Port Adelaide 5015
www.ginninderrapress.com.au

Contents

5

Foreword

It was a drowsy summer afternoon in Melbourne. I had escaped the humidity of the Northern Territory and, thanks to Freya Mathews' generosity, I was staying with her while in town. I was settling in to enjoy every minute of the first afternoon when, suddenly, a deep-throated noise the like of which I had never heard came through the window, sending alarms throughout my system. The noise became more urgent, and then the house started to creak and sway. Pookie, the recent porcine addition to Freya's household, was on the move. She had made her way around to the side of the house and from there she had begun assaulting the frame with her battering-ram snout.

I learned that Pookie addressed Freya in this manner every afternoon at about four o'clock. Food was Pookie's great desire, insistence was her forte, and brute strength was her unassailable asset. Pookie was still a young pig but already she had grown huge and was tearing up the stones in the courtyard. Freya struggled to keep her contained, and Pookie refused. Freya struggled to keep her fed, and Pookie demanded more. Most astonishingly, to me, Freya loved that pig. She sang to it and told it stories, speaking to it in the most gentle way, and accepting totally that Pookie was who she was and would always be herself.

Domesticated pigs are not wild animals, but neither are they companions in the usual sense of the term. Pookie had no interest in pleasing Freya, or, as far as I could see, in forming a relationship. She was wholly, completely and forever focused on herself and her desires. Freya was entranced. One of Pookie's charms was 'that she had not noticed that she was born into a world of human sovereignty'. Indeed, Pookie was totally unaware that she was becoming an enormous burden, an impossible responsibility.

In this captivating story of a pig and a philosopher, Freya takes up the narratival mode of exposition that has recently engaged philosophers. Her account of Pookie tells of a human person's love across a huge species boundary. Few pigs have been so fondly and respectfully brought into print. Freya's philosophical commitment to truth leads her into unfashionable conclusions: pigs are not particularly intelligent, she tells us. On the basis of life with Pookie, she finds pigs to be determined, focused and insistent, but not demonstrably smart. Having made that point, Freya goes on to provide a vivid account of Pookie's actual sentience: her sense of self, her joy, her determination, her later dejection and her capacity for remembrance.

We know that love founded in respect means accepting the other in their otherness; how such a relationship works across species boundaries is a relatively unexplored question. Freya did not want to invent Pookie, she had no desire to refashion the pig's identity or to invent a personality that was untrue to Pookie. Rather, Freya wanted to be close to her, to get to know her, to share a life with her. This is exactly what she did, until it became impossible. And so she asks questions about inter-species commitment: why do people long for relationships with animals?

Freya is Australia's leading eco-philosopher. Her life has been devoted to thinking philosophically and acting ecologically. In the second part of this study, Freya turns to philosophical questions about the relationships between humans and animals, focusing on 'our need for animal company'. Here she is on more speculative ground, ranging across questions of co-evolution, domestication and exploitation. Her commitment to coexistence leads her to imagine a green city of the future designed so that 'mixed communities' can flourish.

Philosophers have for millennia questioned the foundations of reality and the place of humans in that reality. In recent times, with the emergence of eco-philosophy and other branches of environmental/philosophical thought, these questions have taken a relational, dialogical, multi-species, Earth-focused turn. This new approach rests firmly within the actuality of Earth life and the experience of being or becoming part of that actuality. Freya does not hesitate to use words that can seem alarming; 'enchantment' and 'sacredness' are two examples. The point is not to alarm but to entice. We are, Freya affirms, called into love: not the love of fairy tales or of mainstream religions, but rather the love that 'signifies that we belong to an animate order, a pattern of meaning, from which death cannot separate us…'

This 'animate order' that surrounds us, encloses us and responds to us, Freya's book reminds us, for the most part does not come in the easily lovable shape of a companion dog or the stunning beauty and demonstrable cleverness of the dolphin or whale, but in the intractable, erratic, difficult otherness of the pig. Freya guides us along a path that connects Pookie with human–animal ethics and with a radiating love arising from within Earth life. Drawing on her lifelong experience of close relationships with animals, within which Pookie was one interesting episode, Freya evokes for us, and blesses us with, the awe and mystery of life that is radically open to others.

Deborah Bird Rose
Sydney, October 2015

Pookie

Let's imagine spending a moment or two in the Middle Ages. What are the images that come to mind? Turreted castles, ladies in rose-coloured gowns and pointy hats, peasants gathering sheaves of wheat, monks in black cassocks...and pigs! Flick through the pages of any Book of Hours or look at any medieval tapestry and there they are, wandering in alleyways or grubbing for acorns in oak-leafy woods, always in tilted profile, like the animals in bestiaries, and always with that Mona Lisa smile and those knowing human eyes. The jolly pig, rotund and self-satisfied.

Now set those images of the Middle Ages aside, and take a stroll around your local urban neighbourhood. Any pigs about today? Can you hear the clippety-clop of trotters in the shopping mall? Are there snouts in the gutters, muddy wallows where football boots have cut up the soil around the goalposts in the park? Hardly. If you are a city dweller, animals will have pretty much disappeared from your landscape, apart from the odd dog-on-leash or cat-on-porch and a scattering of doughty little street birds.

Pigs are still out there somewhere, of course, as witnessed by the ham and bacon in the nation's fridges. But they are out of sight, sequestered in prison camps that are externally unidentifiable, no longer part of anybody's landscape, anybody's life. Why is this so? Why have pigs, and all the other animals who have figured so essentially in human history, dropped from view? Is this exclusion an integral aspect of modernity? What are the consequences of the rupture of these age-old relations between humanity and its non-human confrères? Could these relations be re-established? Could relations of commensality, for instance, replace those of farming or herding in a contemporary urban context? But what would that imply for our eating habits? Could we, with our current levels

11

of reflexivity, continue to eat animals whose con-specifics were cherished by us as domestic companions? And if we found it intolerable to eat such animals, how would we deal with them when they escaped captivity and turned into feral invaders of our indigenous ecosystems? Is there indeed any place for wildlife, feral or indigenous, in the modern imagination? Is making such a place essential to the ecological revisioning of modernity?

I was given a chance to ponder these questions some years ago when my friend, Julia Bell in Western Australia, airmailed me a six-week-old miniature pig as a birthday present. The arrival of the present was not a complete surprise, though nor was the step to pig ownership a carefully considered one on my part. But after my rash 'yes' to Julia's breathless telephone inquiry as to whether I wanted a piglet for my birthday, I had made the necessary preparations.

These had included writing long letters to my local inner-city council requesting a pig permit and justifying that request. It was the first such application this council had ever received, and pig jokes were flying when I went, in trepidation, into the council offices to discuss the matter with the animal by-laws officer. This was, as it turned out, a charming person named Heather. Heather was an animal nut herself: she had only recently moved into town from a country house she had shared with an amiable pack of dogs and goats and a donkey. I assured Heather that my pig would spend most of the day indoors sitting on the sofa and watching television (though I would have to acquire a television for this purpose – and what a worthy purpose for doing so!). This was my honest expectation.

I had talked to a local breeder of miniature pigs who had dazzled my imagination with his tales of pigs tripping along obediently, collared and leashed, at the heel of their owner by day and companionably watching television with the rest of the family at night. I didn't doubt that my pig would be just like that. Her breeders had estimated that she would grow to 'the size of a kelpie' or about 30 kilograms. Well, our dog, Sashi, was in fact part kelpie, and just about 30 kilograms. She lived very comfortably in our small inner-city backyard, and so would Pookie.

So the day arrived, and I drove out to the airport with my son to fetch the already famous Pookie home. The girls in the air freight depot hummed the tune from the movie *Babe* – then still current – as they carried the container out to us. I was a bit surprised to find that the piglet was black, not pink, as I had imagined. I had only ever seen black pigs in the bush, where they looked very fierce indeed. But Pookie was quiet and polite all the way home, and when we let her out on the veranda she stood demurely in the corner, unapproachable but unfazed. It was Sashi, our dog, who had hysterics, rolling her eyes and looking aghast at the little black stranger, as if at some unholy apparition. For Pookie, however, Sashi was instantly a mother figure and, though maintaining her distance from us, she eagerly sought to attach herself to Sashi's teats.

It was thus in quite a subdued fashion that our life with Pookie began. I thought to myself, 'What a good little girl. The movie got it right. Pigs really are self-possessed creatures, like Babe, polite and composed though assertive in a wholesome way.'

I made up a litter tray and bed with hot-water bottles and blankets on the enclosed veranda at the rear of the house. This would be her home for the moment. When she was toilet trained, she could graduate indoors, to the sofa and the television.

But Pookie spurned the litter tray. The floor of the veranda, sluiced with hot soapy water several times a day, soon showed signs of wood rot. And if the piglet was initially quiet and self-possessed, that was because she had been taking stock. When she felt sure of her new surroundings, the screaming began. Morning and evening, around feeding time, or as soon as anyone stirred inside the house, Pookie started battering at the kitchen door with her long rubbery snout and front hooves, screaming in a voice that sounded like a massacre in a primary school.

The effect was shattering. The dream of the sofa and the television began to collapse, and after a few weeks of sluicing and being battered, I took a firm decision to relocate the Pookster into the backyard rather than into the front parlour. I set up a small shed under an awning by the back door and into it I moved her bed, still full of blankets and hot-water bottles that were recharged several times a day. But now I also added straw, and every day Pookie would artfully make a nest in the straw, lining it with the hot-water bottles and somehow managing to spread the blankets over the top. She would pass the time munching the straw down into a chaff that could be conveniently pressed into all the corners of the shed to shut out draughts. She fastidiously remade that bed a couple of times a day.

Pookie was by now very chummy with my son and me. When we sat outside, she would spring into our laps and push her head up under our jumpers. This was endearing but hazardous for us: while she would doze for a while in our arms, she would soon startle or rally abruptly and her head would fly up. Accidental contact with that mallet-like skull could dislocate the jaw of anyone making the mistake of cuddling up cheek to cheek with her.

The screaming continued. The breeders had explained that if one wanted a pig to remain miniature, one would have to restrict its food intake. It seems hard to credit in retrospect that I could have accepted this, but so crucial was scale to the whole venture that I followed the breeders' dietary guidelines to the letter. But how to keep a pig on a diet happy? I added large quantities of bran to her small ration of pig pellets and Weetbix; a stack of lucerne hay kept her occupied for at least an hour each morning and night as she licked up every last dried clover leaf with an adroit tongue. But still she protested. I started trawling the neighbourhood for greengrocer waste.

What an amazing bounty I found outside nearby supermarkets. Why wasn't somebody collecting all this and converting it into compost? The ecological fallibility of the market, of the law of supply and demand! But such fallibility was, in this case at any rate, working to my advantage, though I had to be persistent. None of the stores could tell me just when their skips would be filled. So I had to prowl, maintain a perennial vigilance. Then, there it would be! A truckload of lettuce or cabbage leaves, and on luckier days, rarer treasures: crates of over-ripe tomatoes or mangoes, scatterings of bruised plums or blemished bananas. On occasion, in summer, I would even alight upon an entire watermelon.

With what triumph I would bear my bags of booty home and with what satisfaction I would watch my Pookie devour the contents. To witness her demolishing a watermelon would make me laugh out loud. First she would breach the rind with her snout, then she would plant her two front feet inside the shell, sucking the juice noisily before chomping through the whole thing, rind and all, from the inside out. Her enjoyment was unqualified. She would tilt her nose at the sky and close her eyes as she gobbled the food with her mouth open, pink juice and squish running down her cheeks. Watching the Pookster eat was more fun than one's own eating!

I started foraging down at the local creek, joining the Italian ladies with their bundles of wild greens. I gathered dandelion leaves and armfuls of a yellow-flowered weed related to chicory and broccoli, the kind of thing we could eat ourselves if times were lean. I was enjoying my role as a forager and relishing my little forays into feraldom. My activities on Pookie's behalf were placing me in new company, not only that of the Italian ladies by the creek but, at the skips, that of bag ladies, scavenging for their own needs, and all manner of colourful crazies indentured to bantams and rabbits and other, more bizarre pets. Keeping this company didn't do much for my prestige, but the thrill of the treasure hunt outweighed the social costs.

Still, pig owning is definitely not for the image-conscious: when shoppers in the car park started offering to let me wheel their trolleys back to the stores to collect the refund, even I had second thoughts.

Actually, I had never noticed before that bag ladies and people in funny hats with bantams riding on the backs of their bikes frequented the shopping centres. I had assumed that in our commercial age these figures out of Bruegel and Bosch had vanished from public view. But foraging for Pookie opened up new windows on reality for me, and there they were, the pre-modern faces. Their teeth uncapped, their warts and moles intact, their heads wrapped in handkerchiefs, they were still laughing to themselves at the margins of the village, just behind the gleaming facades of commerce. I could focus on them and know them now because I was seeing the world through eyes attuned to new registers of salience – to piggy concerns.

Daily life under Pookie's reign was contained within cast-iron routines. As soon as I awoke each morning – and there was no question of sleeping in – I donned my pig gear, which consisted of gumboots and layers of long pink and purple hippie skirts to protect my legs from black hoofprints and mud kisses. In this flowing and voluminous, pre-modern garb, I headed down to the kitchen to prepare the steaming breakfast mash. Hysterical stuck-pig cries accompanied my every move from the other side of the door. But soon the protesting little mouth was stopped, and the round of Pookie chores begun.

Manure, which was always deposited in a particular corner of the yard, had to be collected, hay fetched, the water bucket scrubbed and refilled. Pookie would decline the bucket once the water had become sullied, even when it was her own snout that had done the sullying. Both bucket and water had to be pristine before she would deign to drink.

After breakfast, before hay time and the daily peanut hunt, it was tummy time. Just one tickle was enough, and thump, down she would go, ready for her rub. Each fat little leg would be daintily lifted backward or forward to ensure that you could reach the whole expanse of her tummy, and as you rubbed or brushed – sometimes with a scrubber, sometimes with a straw broom – she would stretch out her neck and close her long-lashed eyes with bliss. I would also groom her sides and comb the tassel of her tail, telling her stories and singing nursery rhymes as I brushed. Her favourite was *The Owl and the Pussycat*. '…and there in a wood a piggywig stood, with a ring in the end of his nose, his nose, with a ring in the end of his nose'. In the evening, before dark, the whole routine would be repeated. I had to be there. There was no question of missing or even of delaying a feed, no matter how pressing my other engagements. Had I done so, the whole of Brunswick, roused by massacre noises, would have been on my doorstep demanding an explanation.

Despite the rigours, life was sweet that spring. To arrive home to a small pig standing on her hind legs at the side gate beside a dog in the same stance invariably lifted my heart. The sound of hoofbeats galloping up the side path lent an edge of brumby wildness to the air of inner-city Brunswick. And Pookie's sauciness, with her black stockings, patent leather high heel hooves and wiggly bottom, could dispel the gloomiest mood. But sweetest of all, and fairest compensation for the trials I endured, were the times when I crawled into her shed at night, and sat in the straw amongst the increasingly flabby hot-water bottles, her dozing head in my lap. The city, the pain of the past, all my many disappointments seemed then to fall away…

Sashi took a less sanguine view of the new arrangements. Pookie adored Sashi, but Sashi continued to be appalled at the intrusion of this black hobgoblin into her domain. At first I was afraid that Sashi might bite Pookles, but these worries soon seemed quaint. As she grew rapidly bigger, comparable in size to Sashi, Pookie's idea of an affectionate tussle was to turn Sashi upside down then stomp on her upturned belly with all four hooves. Pookie found this tremendously funny, but Sashi crawled away from these piggy pranks terrorised and bleeding.

As Pooks was also digging up the brick paving and ringbarking the trees, having torpedoed everything else in the garden, it seemed that the time had come for an enclosure of some kind. So my son fenced off an elongated area beside and behind the house. The run included her shed, and once she had adjusted to the confinement, she seemed entirely happy again. A large area in which to romp would certainly have been welcome to her, but closer to the top of her hierarchy of needs were food, a cosy bed and a wallow. Companionship did rank somewhere on her list, but she was reticent on this point. She had by now outgrown cuddling, and had never been a sentimentalist. Besides, having been assigned a space of her own, she became territorial about it, and was liable to give me a shove with that lethal head if I lingered too long on her side of the fence. But low-key, pottering-about-in-the-backyard kind of companionship, 'each to their own but doing it together', seemed to make for a contented pig.

Pookie had by this stage become a topic of conversation rather favoured by me. I secretly enjoyed astounding new acquaintances with casual references to my pig. I found I could keep whole tables of people amused for hours with Pookie anecdotes. Pig was, if not chic, at least droll. But I was surprised at how opinionated people were on the subject. I myself had never had anything whatever to do with pigs before Pooks erupted into my life, and I knew that the vast majority of people were in the same position. Yet the moment the subject of pigs was broached, everyone declared, 'Pigs are so intelligent!' Everyone. This was always delivered as a statement, never a question, and no one was interested in whether I, as one who consorted with pigs, had a dissenting opinion.

I realised I was witnessing an unconscious instance of ideological conviction. Why was everyone so convinced of pigs' superior intelligence when scarcely anyone in the Western world has shared a household with a pig since the Middle Ages? Our language still carries pig lore accrued from the time when folk did cohabit with their porcine charges. 'As greedy as a pig', 'pig out', 'snouts in the trough'. All true! In the entire universe no one could adore food more than Pookie did. 'Pig-headed'. Yes. Pookie wanted her own way and expected to get it. She butted anyone who obstructed her. 'Male chauvinist pig' and 'pig cop'. Yes. Unflattering as these analogies were to pigs, it was undeniable that Pookie put herself first and showed very little consideration, even by cross-species standards, for the feelings of others. But 'smart as a pig?' I hadn't heard that one. 'Cunning as a pig?' Not that one either. When Pookie wanted something, she used crash power, rather than a calculus, to get it.

So from whence had this universal attribution of intelligence come? I had found Pookie to be in no way comparable to a dog, despite pig breeders' beguiling assurances. Judging from my own experience, pigs cared nothing for their owner's approval. There was no slinking away, tail between legs, following a scolding. When I scolded Pookie, she became infuriated and retaliated with a feisty sideswipe or two. Praise did not even register on her relevance spectrum. There was therefore no way she would be induced to cooperate in an intelligence test – except by bribes. She would, it was true, jump through burning hoops if a jelly bean were in the offing. But it would be difficult to draw inferences from this alacrity. The prospect of a jelly bean would activate every one of her neural pathways right down to the roots of the reptilian brain. For a packet of jelly beans, she could probably solve the field equations for the General Theory of Relativity. But was this a case of brain power or motivation, of endowment or of making much of little? How much is 'intelligence' a function of appetite in any case? An interesting question...

I was at this stage contemplating a series of personal growth workshops, with Pookie as workshop leader. This pig was without question a paragon of self-esteem. She knew her own mind. Her priorities were in order. It mattered nothing to her what others thought of her. She expected her needs to be met. She was queen of her universe: the sun, moon and stars, together with her loyal human subjects, revolved around her. How she relished life – just the life processes themselves, eating and excreting, sunning and sleeping, snorkelling in mud and sifting through chocolate-crumble soil with that moist and mobile snout. Such unmediated joy of life has long been impossible for our civilised selves, and how could we who have lost it disappoint it in one who still possesses it?

I thought that the principal client group for the workshops could be philosophers. Living with Pookie had, in my mind, cast doubt on Socrates' maxim that it is better to be a philosopher dissatisfied than a pig satisfied.

Pookie snorted her contempt for all things reflective and speculative. 'I want life!' she squealed. 'And I want it now! What's more,' she added, with a stamp of her hoof, 'I deserve to get what I want. The world was created specifically for my pleasure. The fish of the sea and the fowl of the air and every creeping thing that creepeth upon the earth was born to wait on me.'

What purpose did it serve to reflect on things, to spend precious time thinking instead of savouring the inexhaustible delights of the given? What purpose indeed. But of course no misfortune had ever yet befallen Pooks. Nothing had yet transpired to dent her confidence in the established scheme of things. She was unaware, for instance, that three million of her kind existed in steel cages behind closed doors in the countryside. She had no inkling that, far from having the upper hand in her domestic affairs, she could, despite her bossiness, be despatched by me at any moment.

Nevertheless, it was salutary to bask in the company of one who was not only precopernican but prelapsarian; I was sure that my hog therapy for anxious philosophers would be a winner.

Was it coincidental, I wondered, that a creature with such supreme self-esteem should, in recent times, have suffered the greatest abasement at human hands? Is factory farming the revenge of modernity on a species which embodies pre-modern elan and self-infatuation? And mightn't all that political correctness – the pigs-are-so-intelligent mantra – emanate from a still-unconscious guilt at the enormity of our human crime against the blithe spirit of the pig?

Not that Pookles was without her Achilles hoof. Although fearless in daytime situations – turning head-lowered, glowing-eyed to any perceived threat – her nerves could get the better of her at the fall of night. Burrowed deep into bales of straw inside her shed, with only the flouncy tassel of her tail protruding, she could erupt vertically at a sudden noise: ancestral predators obviously still stalked the Pookster's dreams.

Despite all my dietary precautions, this irrepressible pig continued to grow. At six months she was as tall as the projected kelpie, but as long as three kelpies. The narrow run beside the house was now inadequate. Besides, both the house and fence were succumbing to Pookie's alarmingly increasing strength. My son filled the excavations she made around the stumps of the house with bluestone pitchers, but although I could barely lift them, Pookie thought nothing of digging them out with her snout then tossing them contemptuously aside. She was loosening the weatherboards on the walls and working on the gas and water pipes. Gaps were starting to appear between the palings, and one day my startled neighbour, Maria, was joined by Pookie at her washing line. Quick thinking with an apple on my part succeeded in luring her back.

It was becoming obvious that in order to avoid wholesale demolition we would have to construct a proper pig pen. We cleared a corner at the far end of the yard, where a shed on a concrete base already stood, and with bags of cement and lengths of four-by-four red gum, my son built a sturdy post and rail fence. When a shiny new pail was wired to a stake and a couple of bales of straw were strewn in the shed, Pooks was very amenable to her new quarters. The pen was shaded by an apple tree and summer windfalls were already abundant. I was watched closely and entreated with urgent grunting as I gathered the windfalls up for her each morning. There was just room in the yard for a toilet corner, a wallow, a dining area and a sunning spot, in addition to her bed, which she took hours each day to make and remake, sealing the tiniest cracks with munched straw and contouring the sleeping hollow to her liking.

Our routine was now re-established. I would muck out the pen morning and evening and lay fresh straw. I stored the manure in big compost bins and applied it to my vegetable plot at CERES (Centre for Education and Research in Environmental Strategies), our local environment park. Elixir to vegetables, this pig manure was the secret behind the mysteriously towering broccoli and zucchini in my plot. I brought the leaves and leftovers back home to Pooks. At last I had discovered a place for pigs in sustainable agriculture – not as meat but as compost kits. Feed in at one end all the available green waste in your neighbourhood and remove, from the other end, pure gold. Nor was this the only role I could envisage for Pookie in the new economy: I schemed endlessly with my inventor friend from CERES, Bill, about setting up a methane plant in the backyard. Bill was the keeper of the methane digesters at CERES. We fantasised about summer nights boiling an outdoor kettle on a cooker rigged up from a forty-four-gallon drum and run on Pookie power.

Although the new pen was a lot more miniature than she was, Pookles now seemed very content. The constellations continued to revolve around her. Visitors to the house were immediately ushered into her presence, where they invariably gasped gratifyingly at her enormous size, her sheer amazingness. She basked in the praise, which was only her due, after all.

Ku, our little duck, and Rosie, the galah, kept her company. She would call to Sashi, who sometimes consented to play rough with her, as in the old days, but from the safe side of the fence. Occasionally Sashi would stand with an ambivalent expression on her face and allow Pookie to lick her rump with her greedy little tongue.

Pookie plainly enjoyed my company but because I was her provider she was always impatient when I appeared. The very sight of me seemed to make her angry that the goods and services were not reaching her faster. So I did sometimes feel taken for granted.

In the winter of that first year, I had to attend a conference in the United States. My son had kindly agreed to stand in for me as Pookie's minder (slave!). While I was away, I had a lucid dream of arriving home and going out into the backyard, which was preternaturally bright and flowery in the dream; Pookie ran to greet me with a series of excited little grunts so affectionate they pierced my heart. But no such welcome awaited me on my actual return. If anything, Pookie seemed disgruntled at my absence.

But this surliness soon passed, and with the pig in the sty and the new routines in place, things at last began to settle down. Pookie no longer screamed. The backyard positively purred with her benign and gratified emanations. Had we known that she was going to reach the size of a young hippopotamus rather than a kelpie, we would have penned her from the start and saved ourselves a lot of stress. But now that the difficulties were finally over, I began, perversely enough, to have serious doubts. I lived in dread of a breakout.

The Pookster's size and strength inexorably increased. Our constructions continually turned out to be inadequate, calling for further improvisations. The post and railing fence had to be reinforced with industrial mesh. Gaps started to appear between the palings behind the bamboo hedge. I laced the hedge with barbed wire. But would the old shed stand up to the heavings and hoings now taking place within it?

One afternoon I found the yard seemingly vacant – no eager wet snout poking through the rails, no startled snort as a dozing pig awoke to the sound of my approach. When I got closer to the pen, there seemed to be half a pig lying in front of the shed – and a very flat half, at that, its tail flicking with excitement. In response to my anguished cry, the whole pig emerged backwards from a gigantic excavation. Large chunks of concrete had been tossed up into the pen. It seemed she had been working on the base of the shed from underneath. I spent a frantic half-hour wrestling bluestone pitchers into the hole before refilling it. One of them jammed my hand, bruising it badly.

I lay awake at night imagining Pookie's snout working its way through the fence palings, her head at last bursting through, unseen, into George and Tessia's yard next door. My mind recoiled at images of Pookie ripping the tops off George's tomato plants, Pookie ploughing the immaculate lawn, tugging at washing, knocking over pot plants. And this was the merest beginning! Now I could see other backyards trashed, Pookie trotting out triumphant onto the street. People were scattering in terror; there were accidents, pile-ups. Pookie was marauding up Lygon Street, derailing trams, upsetting bicycles and prams, storming cafés, ramping up against the cake counter in the *pasticceria* and gobbling the handmade chocolates from the shelf. Pookie everywhere, amusing herself recklessly, without limit. I saw myself ruined, my house seized, my shoulders stooped before a lifetime of debt. I felt an avalanche of public outrage pouring down on my sleepless head…

For months I wrestled with these secret worries, but eventually I came to the conclusion that, much as we loved Pookalina and enjoyed indulging her, it was necessary to think about alternative arrangements.

Even the prospect of relocating her, however, posed hair-raising possibilities. How were we to do it? How were we to manoeuvre her through the front gate without her breaking loose? If only she were broken to collar and leash! But our attempts to tie her to the pole of the Hills hoist in order to habituate her to the feel of a lead, early in the piece, had led to an ECG for me, such was the volume of her screaming. (Truly. The decibel level of a screaming pig is said to be higher than that of a jet at take-off, and twenty times more stressful in its expressiveness. Pains in the chest had become a regular occurrence for me.)

Even if we were somehow to funnel her up the side path to the front gate, how were we to coax her into a waiting vehicle? Wouldn't she just, with a toss or two of that death-dealing skull, breach our feeble defences and launch herself into my nightmare scenario? Wouldn't it be safer and easier simply to keep reinforcing the pen and allow her to live out her fifteen-year lifespan there? After all, there were certain advantages in lodging a pig. Not only was she a compost-making kit; she was also a security device. Any intruder who dropped into our backyard in the dead of night was in for a richly deserved shock! But still, my mind would not rest. I shadow-boxed endlessly with the problem.

Meanwhile, the Pookster basked, demanding more, and yet more, petulantly, never pausing to offer thanks, but giving joy nonetheless.

To find a home for a porcine prima donna whose claim to miniature status could no longer be upheld was no small task. I was willing to finance a pension for the rest of her life if a pig-care establishment could be found. But how to endear her to prospective carers? How to explain to anyone who had not changed her hot-water bottles at eight weeks and taught her the *Owl and the Pussycat* that the charm of this piggywig lay precisely in the fact that she had not noticed that she was born into a world of human sovereignty.

In any case, wherever a vacancy for a miniature pig might conceivably exist, it was by now filled. I checked out all the children's farms around town. Stories of battered ex-owners abounded. One pig at Bundoora – a fetching little white-haired sow – had been brought in after ripping the door off the fridge. The owner had returned home one day to find the pig standing on its hind legs half inside the smashed fridge, with a yoghurt carton on its head and ice cream and raw eggs dripping from its whiskers.

My secret dream was for Pooks to be adopted by CERES. The CERES site included a children's farm, and the animals were a motley collection of giveaways and foundlings. The current star at the stables was Peggy Sue, a five-year-old sow who dwarfed the young Pookster. Two rare-breed ginger pigs, Dennis and Rita, only slightly smaller than Peggy Sue, were also in residence, with a brood of piglets. Chris, the animal farm coordinator, was of the firm view that CERES did not require another pig, but I disagreed. What a great arrangement for a cash-strapped community organisation, I argued warmly, to have a pig on a pension!

As luck would have it, Dennis and Rita happened to catch the eye of a rare-breed fancier at just that moment and were signed up for a new life, once Rita's piglets were weaned. So the longed-for vacancy had eventuated. I doubled my lobbying efforts with the CERES management committee, and before long Pookie was in! Chris was less than enthused, but I hoped that my piggy's cheeky charm would eventually win him over.

Although relieved and elated at Pookie's acceptance by CERES, I awaited removal day with dread. I phoned Christian, Pookles' personal physician, and asked him to attend. It had taken me a long time to track down an urban vet who was up to pigs, but Christian, who hailed from a clinic on the edge of town, was a young Indiana Jones of a vet. Slight but fearless, with a little black braid at the back of his head and cowboy boots, he was ready to wrestle any pesky beast to the ground. As soon as he arrived, he administered a hefty tranquilliser and while we waited for Chris over the next twenty minutes, we watched the Pookster gradually capsize. (Chris had been adamant that a tranquilliser was unnecessary, but this was the conviction of a man who had not yet had the pleasure of actually meeting Pooks.)

When Chris eventually joined us, we erected some makeshift barriers. Paper barriers, to my anxious eyes. Rainer, my son, then opened the gate to the pen. I had a watermelon at the ready, and a back-up supply of mangoes and peanuts. Pookie's out-of-focus eyes widened at the sight of the temptations and she rushed, as fast as her slow-motion state would allow, out of the enclosure. Rainer directed her with the watermelon, and Christian and Chris encouraged her from the rear. She staggered the entire length of the side path, squealing all the while, but when she reached the front of the house she sank, taking Rainer, who had his arms around her neck, with her. The two of them lay together in a crumpled heap for a while, puffing, Rainer and I both half-crying, until we all managed to revive Pook's interest in the watermelon.

Chris had backed a trailer-cage up to the front gate, and now we pushed and petted and begged her to mount the ramp. There was only the smallest space between the gatepost and the trailer, but just as I had feared, Pookie, even in her befuddled state, did her utmost to break through the barrier of arms and legs and make a freedom dash. Somehow, between us, however, we deflected that battering ram of a head and heaved her up the ramp and into the trailer, which was soon dripping with squashed fruit. Along the street, people had appeared and gathered in little knots, staring silently.

Oh, the sadness of seeing the unsteady little figure looking back at me as the vehicle, driven by Chris, with Rainer on board, drew away. The sadness and the relief. For eighteen months that beady-eyed parcel of elemental power had ruled our lives, but now she was launched into the wide world, a world unimaginably unsafe for even the most recalcitrant pig. Her fate was still partly in my hands, but the thread of connection between us would from here on become tenuous. I could soothe her and stroke her ears through the transition period, but her story was no longer tied to mine. Oh Pookie, unmanageable, monstrous but so-vulnerable child…

Things did not go well for Pook over the first days, weeks and even months of her new life. She was housed in a large but dark stall in the animal stables, and her status sank from queen of the universe, sun at the centre of the firmament, to mere animal amongst animals. No longer did she enjoy fresh straw every day for her bed or muck-outs twice a day. No longer did anyone care that she had sullied her drinking water with her snout and needed a sparkling fresh refill; the same slimy water was topped up day after day. Sackloads of fresh treats from the fruit and vegetable skips no longer dropped at her feet for morning and afternoon tea. She was not even a main attraction. Peggy Sue, being a quiet and well-mannered pig as well as twice Pookie's size, was undisputed box office star, and although Peg died soon after Pookie's arrival, top billing passed to Rita and her red piglets. Both Dennis and Rita were much larger than Pookalina, and the schoolchildren who visited the stables in their scores each day, on educational outings, would hurry past Pookie in their eagerness to see the 'really big pig'. In fact, a lot of people who passed by did not even notice the little Pookster in her corner – a black pig in a dark poke.

Pookie grieved. Overnight she had undergone her very own copernican revolution. Ejected from the centre of the universe, she was thrust out to ignominy on the edges. Truly she had believed that pigs ruled the world, that humans existed only as devotees for pigs. How rudely that illusion was now shattered. And the world was so much bigger and busier than little Pookles had imagined. There were so many people, so many animals, a cast of thousands, so much going on. No longer did everyone who came into her field of view hurry toward her, exclaiming at her size, her sheer amazingness. Instead, they passed her by, hundreds of them, laughing and joshing amongst themselves, ignoring her, sometimes even making crude sausage jokes at her expense. Oh Pookie! How could they be so heartless!

She lay in her stall with her back to visitors. At first she raised her head each time excited voices approached. But eventually she lost any hope that the excitement might be on her account, and she lay unmoving as the voices came and went.

Nor did her new keepers take kindly to her. Her normal bossiness had degenerated into snappiness, and the volunteers were scared of her. A 'firm hand' was brought into play. But a firm hand had never made any impression on Pookie. I had tried smacking her in her tantrum days, only to succeed in almost fracturing my hand and enraging her. The way into the Pookster's good graces – the only way – was through shameless bribery. For pig-headed though she was, her free will melted at the prospect of a Smartie. The length of black hose that Chris used to guide her around the yard made her sulky and defiant.

I visited her every day, with scaled-down quantities of her former treats, and an array of different brushes and brooms with which to groom and pamper her. Suddenly she was visibly thrilled to see me. The queen of the universe would hurry over to the fence, talking ten to the dozen, when she heard my call. 'Oomp, oomp oomp oomp oomp,' she would burble, her face brightening, her wet snout searching my hands for peanuts.

If she were out in the paddock, she would break into a run at the sight of me and would arrive with a skid, grunting and chattering. As I greeted her, nose to nose through the wire, she would sometimes actually lift her head and open her mouth wide in a kind of excited barking. She was eager for her titbits, of course, but this was more than titbit talking; this was serious social excitation. She would continue that strange excited barking even after the titbit bag was empty.

This was exactly the way she had greeted me in the dream in Boston; the dream had been prescient. The heart-melting enthusiasm of that greeting was now my daily reward for eighteen months of indenture. If I were unable to enter the paddock or her enclosure, she would flop down as close as possible to the fence so that I could crouch on hands and knees and reach through the wire to scrub her tummy. She would close her eyes, as of old, and I would recite the *Owl and the Pussycat* as I stroked, praying that no one would walk past and surprise me in this eccentric attitude.

But despite my devoted visits, Pookie desponded. The flies worried her. Her less-than-pristine conditions demoralised and depressed her. Her hair fell out. Skin afflictions erupted. She was moved into a more salubrious outdoor pen, but Rita's bullying in the paddock caused her to pull muscles, and soon she was lame as well as bald. In the weekends I sometimes found stones in her pen, thrown by young out-of-hours tormentors.

How the mighty had fallen. How the world had turned, from her oyster to a slough of despond, a vale of disillusionment. Her piggy heart, so ill-adapted to reflection, lay in a ruined state for six long months. Her beady eye grew dull, her condition dirty. I grieved for her, but I knew that so long as she could weather the transition, life at CERES offered the best prospect for her. She could not live in a backyard in Brunswick, and alternative options were scarce. If she could only win people's hearts, attract a new circle of admirers, the moon and the stars could eventually be drawn back into her orbit.

After six months, Demeter, presiding goddess at CERES (Ceres being the Roman version of the Greek deity), took pity on Pookie. Pigs are sacred to Demeter, and there came a point at which the goddess could no longer bear the sight of her little charge, by nature so jovial, reduced to such a state of abjection. A wind of change blew through the stables.

Political troubles had long been brewing, and Pook had been caught in the emotional crossfire of undeclared hostilities. Now regime change occurred, amidst political fireworks. Chris and his assistant left. A new animal coordinator, part of a larger team with a new and ambitious vision for an organic farm at CERES, took over. Pookie found herself in the care of a beautiful man with silver-fox curls whose background was in dance and biodynamics and Steiner principles rather than the 'firm hand' school of farming. Martin believed in animal souls; he understood that Pookie was indeed queen of the universe, that she needed to be spoiled and indulged. He pledged himself to her gallantly as loyal subject and squire, while still keeping a handle on the practicalities of her everyday requirements.

She was bathed regularly and cleaned, fed an organic diet, and moved to a leafy enclosure with a nice private concrete boudoir to which she could retreat when tired of the attentions and jibes of passers-by. Her skin cleared up and her hair regrew. A spring returned to her step, and the air of sullen defiance that had settled on her gave way to the old swagger of naughtiness. Pookie was, not in love exactly – an impossibility for a pig – but gratified. Even I found myself tangled up in a shadowy oedipal triangle. If Pookie had terrorised her way into my psyche as my child, admittedly monstrous, but all the more consuming for that, then who was this new figure who had entered the unconscious parental contract, if not...? For months I was in the grip of these strange oedipal undercurrents, and giant pigs and silver goat-men cavorted and shape-shifted in my dreams with an insistency that confounded my reality principle.

However, now that Pookie was back on her feet, I could allow her to recede a little from my life. With Martin as her knight and champion, and her own improved morale, she began at last to attract the longed-for circle of admirers. Indeed, she was becoming famous in the neighbourhood. So my visits became less frequent and at the same time more enjoyable.

There ensued an idyllic phase, during which I dropped into CERES two or three times a week, both to tend my vegetable plot and to visit my beloved child, who was now, if not as puffed up as once she was, at least content and mild. CERES really was mine during that phase. Having

Pookie on site, as well as my plot, gave me an inner link to it that made it the mythic centre of my psyche as well as the focus of my bio-regional vision. It was the place, it seemed, to which I had been always coming home. But such dreams are hard to sustain in the context of modern society, and after this joyous interlude, Demeter's gentle gusts of change began to blow again.

Although the new regime at the stables had seen the departure of most of the animals, leaving only Pookie and three of the goats and an assortment of poultry, the stables themselves and one of the two remaining animal paddocks were now earmarked for 'development'. An organic produce garden and a Saturday market were proposed. Any animals that remained would have to be integrated into the management plan – they would have to be organically certified productive members of the farm. No more taking in of giveaways and foundlings now. A free-range same-breed flock of laying chickens – strict professionals – was envisaged, and a couple of Dexter cows, Dexters being a miniature variety, suitable for urban conditions, with a high milk yield. There was no place in this business plan for deluded pigs whose only claim to permaculture status was the production of little steaming piles of poo. Even the goats and ducks and geese would have to go. Despite my impassioned arguments and interventions, Martin could see the wisdom of this plan, and advertised Pookie in the newspaper as free to a good home.

Martin was confident he could screen out pork-eaters from the prospective carers who came forward in response to the advertisement, but I had a much darker view of Pookie's prospects. Once again, I racked my brains for alternatives, and once again fortune, touched by Demeter's hand, smiled. For it just so happened that during the two years Pookie had been at CERES, I had met a man named Peter with a large property up near Hanging Rock. Peter was one of us, an animal nut with a vast menagerie.

Roaming the grounds of Bindara Farm were highland cattle, looking like bison from the American wild west, black-pointed Suffolk sheep, a pair of ostriches named Tony and Narelle, alpacas, Shetland ponies, pheasants and guineafowl roosting high in gum trees, emus, ferrets, joeys, baby wombats, a pack of dogs...and pigs. Three pigs, to be precise. Molly in a leafy chook run, and Jean and Wilber in a shady paddock up the hill. I had been staying off and on, writing, in a little flat that Peter had available for rent on the farm, so I was already on fairly familiar terms with Tony and Narelle and the rest of the crew. I didn't like to impose on Peter's extremely good nature, but this was a moral emergency. So after the dreaded advertisement appeared, I popped the question: could Peter possibly find it in his heart to...um...take in another...um...pig. Peter didn't miss a beat, and quite casually agreed. Oh, the relief! The joy! The eternal gratitude! The horrid ad was abandoned. Pookie was still in the family!

So now another removal was necessary. But this time Martin was in charge. Rainer and I assisted, but I did not bear the responsibility. Besides, about twenty people were there to help and watch the fun. Martin backed a trailer up to the stable yard gate, made a corridor out of straw bales, opened the stall in which Pook was being held, rodeo-style, then ran ahead of her with pellets and potatoes. Pookie followed helplessly. There was some struggle and stumbling at the straw-bale steps up into the trailer, but then – slam, she was in. Martin drove the truck that towed the trailer, and Rainer and I followed in my car, keeping a close eye on Pookalina all the way. She actually lay down in the copious straw that Martin had provided and seemed quite relaxed for someone enjoying the fresh air of the freeway for the first time.

On arriving at Peter's, we had to entice her through three gates and across an emu enclosure into the pig paddock. The pig paddock stretched up an expansive, granite-studded, wooded slope. At the foot of the hill ran a creek in which Jean and Wilber had made enviable wallows. Little marble angels stood about on tree stumps, relics of goodness knows what funerary adventures on Peter's part. Pookie followed Martin across the emu enclosure, paying no attention whatever to the emus crowding and craning over her. When she reached the pig paddock, however, the lure of the wide open spaces proved greater than that of the pellets, and she set out purposefully for the hilltop. A watermelon swiftly re-engaged her attention, and guided her into the little yard where she was to stay until she had successfully completed the protocols with Wilber and Jean. That's where we left her, after a parting tummy rub, lying contently in lush grass in the shade of tall gums. We all went into Peter's kitchen for a cup of tea and a slice of the orange cake that Peter had baked, because it just so happened that it was Martin's birthday.

For a year or so, I continued to stay at Peter's now and again, and I witnessed Pookie's transformation into a quieter and happier pig. Peter didn't believe in putting pigs on diets, organic or otherwise, and dumped a trailer load of leftovers from the local bakery in the pig paddock a couple of times a week. Stale cream buns. Wrinkled chocolate cakes. There was a new serene light in Pookie's eyes as her tummy expanded. In time, she even stopped ambling up to the fence to greet me. With no more need of me, she seemed, to my relief, to have forgotten me, and my visits eventually ceased.

However, early in 2004 I dropped in to visit Peter again. After a cup of tea, we strolled up to the pig paddock. Pookie was standing near the fence and shuffled over when we appeared. She was larger than when I had last seen her, larger even than Wilber, her teats sweeping the ground as she walked. Her corpulence was beautiful, not gross, but cuddly and attractively pear-shaped when she sat down. To my astonishment, she seemed extremely pleased to see me, pressing her snout against my hand – the old mud kisses – while oomp oomp oomping to me excitedly the way she used to do at CERES, though peacefully, without agitation. I thought, well, I might as well try the *Owl and the Pussycat*. So I started reciting, and by the time I reached the bit about the piggywig, clunk, she was down in the dust, her tummy up against the mesh of the fence, ready to be rubbed. Oh Pookie! Who would have thought! Her face wore the old Mona Lisa smile. Her heart was back in its rightful precopernican slot. We could have been standing in a Book of Hours. All was well with the world. It was a tonic to see.

Living With Animals

'Without animals,' says another Peter, a Masai nomad interviewed once in the *New Internationalist*, 'life isn't worth living'.

Even without my love affair with Pookie, I could not be in more heartfelt agreement. I have always lived with animals, and animals have been amongst my closest family members and mentors. I could not imagine my life without them. But how many people today would share this sentiment? For how many would it be football that makes life worth living, or cars, or opera, or ice skating? Is there anything to ground my conviction that the company of animals is a necessary part of social life, in a way that football, cars, opera and ice skating manifestly are not, and that we relinquish or forego this aspect of life at our peril?

There are two parts to this question. The first is, is it important for us, for our own well-being or the realisation of our human potential, that we live in intimate commensal relations with animals? The second is, is it important for the natural environment that we live in such relations? Does the world need us to continue to live in our ancestral communalism with animals?

Is our present estrangement from both the natural world (as evidenced in the environmental crisis) and from ourselves (as evidenced in the intense neuroticisation of life in contemporary 'advanced' societies) due at least in part to the progressive removal of animals from our day-to-day urban reality? Do we then need to find ways of restoring animals to the human household in order to address both the environmental crisis and our own crisis of consciousness?

Our Need for Animal Company

Let's start with the question whether intimate connections with animals are foundational to our human well-being. It is an oft-cited research finding that people who enjoy the day-to-day company of animals are healthier in various respects than people who do not: they tend to visit the doctor less frequently, use less medication, have lower cholesterol and blood pressure levels, recover more quickly from illness and suffer less from feelings of loneliness.

Clearly, inexperienced pet pig owners were not included in these surveys, since judging from my case they would have suffered vastly increased rates of stress and heart attack and sudden death, relative to the general populace. But putting the special hazards of consorting with pigs aside, it has been estimated that pet ownership saves the Australian health care system one and a half billion dollars per year. And even pet pig owners, if they survived the tantrums and tyranny, would share in a set of intangible benefits that arise from an obscure, ill-defined and all-but-forgotten form of…well, love.

What are these benefits, these fillips to our well-being? One of the benefits is that animal company can defuse a lot of the socially generated pressure in our lives. Animals are non-judgemental friends. They do not compete with us. Hence we can relax with them, and enjoy spontaneous affection and cathartic physical closeness: we can 'be ourselves' in the presence of such companions, since they have no socially acquired expectations of us. They offer us emotional and psychological release.

In addition, emotional involvement with creatures who do not share our human goals and aspirations, our systems of values, enables us to gain an external perspective on those values. It enables us to appreciate how odd or arbitrary our human priorities might appear to non-human observers. It is, after all, entirely contingent that there have not evolved on this planet diverse species with mutually communicable forms of intelligence that would enable their members to offer explicit and forceful appraisals of human conduct. As it is, we have to try to imagine the cross-species perspectives from which such critiques would emanate. But when we do so, assisted by the intimacy we acquire with animals through commensality, then socially prescribed imperatives have less hold on us – we can achieve a certain distance from them, a certain detachment. We become less driven, less enslaved to discursive ideals and images, and hence more receptive to our actual bodily and instinctual needs, more self-accepting, with all the implications for health and healing which flow from that.

It does not seem, to me, too far-fetched to speculate that there may even be a direct physiological dependence of humans on animal companionship that would help to explain why people who enjoy that companionship are, by and large (tantrum-induced heart attacks notwithstanding), healthier than others. Some evolutionary theorists argue that our ancestors' early genetic 'contract' with certain animals – particularly dogs – enabled us to develop the characteristics that now mark us as human.

According to this theory, it was our association with dogs – which was initiated at least in part by the dogs themselves, possibly as early as one hundred thousand years ago – which enabled our ancestors to dispense with something that is otherwise mandatory for mammalian predators, namely an acute sense of smell: when dogs agreed to join us in the hunt, they could henceforth do our sniffing for us. The advantage for us of delegating our scenting function in this way was that we could thereby dispense with our muzzle. *Sans* muzzle, we could achieve frontal vision, and hence improved hand-eye coordination, and that in turn was a precondition for the development of our tool-making capability. The retraction of the muzzle also entailed the shrinkage and refinement of the tongue, which thereby became capable of the short, highly differentiated sounds required for speech. According to this theory, then, it was through a functional interdependence with dogs that we became human. The deal for dogs, in this scenario, was of course that they received board and lodgings; history has resoundingly vindicated the proto-dogs' evolutionary choice.

Delectable as this theory is, it overlooks the small detail that other primates have also lost their muzzles, without the assistance of dogs. Since it is nevertheless undeniable that nearly all known human communities have included dogs, some co-evolutionary cooperation between the two species does look plausible: human beings may indeed have evolved some kind of physiological need for contact with dogs. If our age-old compact with dogs rests on certain adaptive benefits, then that compact may be wired in by other more direct, physiological forms of interdependency.

Our bodies may unconsciously respond to subtle canine emanations, just as women's bodies, for instance, unconsciously respond to the subtle menstrual signals emanating from female housemates. If all dogs were banished from our cities – and many indignant citizens are crying out for just such a ban – a massive malaise in the human population might ensue. Such a malaise might take directly physical form, such as immunological decline: the evidence that raising children without exposure to ('dirty') animals tends to weaken their immune systems, where this renders them susceptible to allergies, counts in favour of this kind of interpretation. But the malaise might also take more psychological form – it might be more akin to the depression which is already endemic in our relatively animal-free 'advanced' industrial civilisations. It might manifest as a vague sense of incompleteness or meaninglessness, leading to emotional neediness and compensating material acquisitiveness. Or it might be experienced as an existential loneliness which no amount of intra-species socialising can assuage.

Consider the latter possibility for a moment. If we have lived in intimate community with dogs and other animals for anything up to a hundred thousand years, wouldn't it be likely that we would have a distinct psychological need for their company, a need that could not be satisfied by human substitutes? Anyone who habitually walks in open spaces with a close canine friend can testify to the unique appropriateness of dogs as walking companions. Bounding along with infectious interest and joy in their surroundings, they leave us free – free to think our own thoughts and to observe those surroundings keenly ourselves – while nevertheless staying faithfully within our orbit, maintaining an unobtrusive closeness with us.

Additionally, anyone who has spent time in Aboriginal settlements can testify to the feeling of comfort that dog packs lend to a community, provided of course that the dogs are not themselves a source of danger. Their constant mingling with the people, their presence at meetings and their forays onto the football field, their barking and carrying on amongst themselves on the margins of human activities, add a safe, convivial and companionable dimension to life.

Small pot-bellied pigs (genuine 'miniatures', excluded from Australia by quarantine laws) provide this dimension of conviviality in the villages of Papua New Guinea and other parts of south-east Asia. Horses do it in Outer Mongolia, camels in northern India, holy cows in India. Even to sit in the garden with an affectionate duck tugging at one's shoelaces can afford a uniquely peaceful interlude in the daily round.

In light of the emotional and psychological satisfactions that we have experienced for thousands of years in the wider social world of the 'mixed community' of humans and animals, then, isn't it reasonable to assume that, deprived of these satisfactions, we moderns might feel unfulfilled and obscurely lonely, even if we have never experienced these satisfactions at first hand, for ourselves. And mightn't this unfulfilment and loneliness contribute to the social malaise of modern life?

So perhaps it is important for our own well-being to continue the ancient human tradition of living in mixed households or communities. But why might it be important for the natural environment itself that we honour and maintain our ancestral commensal links with animals?

Why Nature Needs Us to Live in Company with Animals

If animal companions do indeed help to make us less driven, competitive and acquisitive, then their presence in our lives works against the world-destroying ethos of contemporary economics, with its competitive individualism and consumerism.

If animals help to bring us down to earth, deflating our modern ambitions and pretensions by exposing them to inter-species scrutiny, then we shall be less anxious to remain in the scramble for success, wealth and power, where this scramble, on a mass scale, is driving the engines of the great bulldozer that is our present economy.

Indeed, to the extent that we share our lives with animals, we shall not only be less willing but less able to adapt to the regime of efficiency and control which is a prerequisite of capitalist production: animals constantly disrupt our life and work with unpredictable contingencies – escapes, fights, sudden illnesses, injuries, embarrassing lapses. They bring an element of slapstick and anarchy into the cool, smart, self-absorbed world of business and public affairs. They make us miss work; they muss up the perfect clothes, perfect hair, that are needed to assure our 'professionalism', our presentability, in this public world; they strew shit and dirt around the manicured gardens, and leave paw marks through the tidy houses, that announce our hard-won social status.

While this can admittedly be stressful, it does gently lead us back from the obsessive quest which is definitive of the modern ethos and which is at the root of the environmental crisis: the quest to usurp and transcend nature, to place ourselves above and beyond its reach, to inhabit a kind of glossy advertiser's version of Plato's heaven, in which moth and rust do not corrupt, because they are kept at bay by chemical warfare, and where thieves do not break in and steal, because the place is patrolled by security guards. In other words, by staying in touch with our animal kin, we stand a greater chance of seeing through the dangerous illusions of a world increasingly dedicated to economic ideals of wealth, power and success that are defined in stark opposition to, or at the expense of, the natural environment.

Another reason why, as environmentalists, we should encourage commensal relations between animals and people, especially children, is that such relations presumably help to engender human empathy towards animals in general, including those in the wild.

When people discover the unique personalities and communicative capabilities of their animal friends and familiars, they are logically drawn to credit other animals with such potentialities too, and to extend to them, in principle, a degree of consideration commensurate with that which, they have realised, is due to the animals of their acquaintance. In this way, as is well recognised, animal companions can serve as 'ambassadors' for animal life generally, awakening in us new levels of awareness and responsibility vis-à-vis the natural world.

It must be admitted, however, that this ambassador argument is, prima facie, open to objection. In the first place, what of those rural folk, whom we have all encountered, who have been in contact with animals throughout their lives yet who nevertheless treat all animals as totally inconsiderable robots? Then there are the people who enjoy family relationships with particular, privileged animals, yet continue to handle the rest with callous indifference. How are we to account for the fact that daily contact with animals has not, in these instances, led to a more considerate attitude towards animals in general?

One way of accounting for this is via the hypothesis that it was the fact of domestication itself, in its more grossly instrumental forms, which led to our cultural objectification of animals. That is, according to some theorists, in drawing animals into our domiciliary space, and raising them within the circle of the human clan, then slaughtering them for food or other purposes, we in fact violated the taboo against violence towards kin. The moral gravity of this transgression required that we rationalise our action by denying the moral significance of domestic – and by extension, all other – animals, reducing them to the status of objects that may be produced and consumed without the slightest compunction. In other words, to justify the utilisation of animals raised, like kin, within the human circle, we invented an ideology of animals as objects, which effectively closed our eyes to their otherwise manifest subjectivity.

Ideology unquestionably can blind us to the subjectivity of others, as is plainly attested by the phenomena of slavery, racism and sexism in the human context. So the mere fact that we keep 'pets', or come into daily contact with other animals, will not of itself ensure that we develop empathy for them.

Communication between self and other can occur only when occlusive ideologies have been exposed and removed. For companion animals to serve as moral ambassadors for the animal world at large, then, prima facie anthropocentric prejudices have first to be set aside. But when we do set them aside, and begin to discover the rich, subjectivity-charged presence and particularity of familiar animals, then not only will the absurdity of these prejudices be exposed, but the long journey to a new moral universe, a richly variegated universe of moral beings, can begin.

If it is accepted that companion animals do induce in us a new moral seriousness about animals generally, then a question arises concerning the status of domestic animals used for productive purposes. Does our new moral seriousness condemn the utilisation of animals for such purposes? If so, is it really in the interests of the species in question, since those species at present owe their very existence to the fact that they are so utilised? How ironical would it be if the dawning of this new moral seriousness led not to an animal renaissance, but to the further retreat of animals both from their present evolutionary strongholds and from our own lives!

The question, then, is whether it is possible to reconcile empathy for animals with their domestic utilisation. Such reconciliation of empathy and use appears to be possible to the extent that utilisation is of net benefit to the animals concerned. When the animals concerned are considered as species rather than as individuals, it is clear that productive forms of domestication have been of net benefit to them: domestic animals are some of the few animal species still flourishing in a world of declining biodiversity.

However, the kind of empathy induced by intimate relationships with animal companions leads us to consider animals as individuals rather than as mere instances of species. So although reproductive success at the level of species is obviously a necessary condition for an individual's existence, and is in this sense in its interests, it is, equally obviously, not a sufficient condition for the individual's well-being.

To reconcile utilisation with empathy, we need to be assured that the existence that our exploitative intentions confer on an individual domestic animal affords both the experiential opportunities and the requisite lifespan to enable that animal to achieve the form of self-realisation appropriate to its particular kind.

This implies that the use we may justifiably make of animals will vary according to their species: what may be an acceptable use of one species with a particular set of needs and sensibilities may not be acceptable for a species differently endowed. In particular, while humane killing of animals who lack any consciousness of death may be admissible, the killing of animals who understand and fear death, and who grieve for their own dead (as apparently do elephants and chimps), may be completely inadmissible, involving as it would the systematic infliction of intolerable suffering. Such suffering may very well, from the viewpoint of animals themselves, cancel the benefits of being alive. (This is evidenced by the fact that such animals can pine to death when bereaved.)

In short, the fact that domestic utilisation affords evolutionary niches for certain species in a world of disappearing niches seems to be a prima facie reason for regarding such utilisation as compatible with respect. However, a full-blown attitude of empathy – such as we develop through intimate association with animal companions – requires that the forms of utilisation we countenance be compatible with the self-realisation of the animals used, where this implies that different forms and degrees of utilisation will be appropriate for different species.

Moreover, once we acknowledge the moral significance of the animals we use, together with the moral gravity of our practices of utilisation, it would seem to become incumbent on us to develop cultural expressions of respect, gratitude and indebtedness for the lives we have thus dedicated to our own ends. In this way, our conduct towards domestic animals could develop more affinity with the familial attitudes of hunter-gatherer peoples towards the wild species that constitute their prey.

However, when domestic utilisation of animals is subject to such protocols, it may not only be consistent with empathetic concern for the interests of animals: it might actually be required by such concern. As environmentalists, committed to the maximal preservation of non-human life on earth, yet facing the cold, hard fact that in the twenty-first century, the processes of urbanisation and industrialisation that have been synonymous with the disenchantment and tragic devastation of the non-human world are only going to accelerate and intensify, don't we have to admit that one of our best chances for 'saving nature' is by bringing nature back into the human domain?

For the last few centuries, we have witnessed the runaway humanisation of nature; now perhaps it is time to inaugurate the wholesale naturalisation of human habitat. Our cities are one of the major biological habitats of the future, and our task, as environmentalists, is to ensure that they provide the best opportunities for non-human life that we can devise. We can do this partly by increasing the amount of urban habitat for wildlife. Such habitat can be created by way of indigenous plantings and by permacultural programs of food production in the city. Buildings can also be designed or adapted to create, rather than exclude, habitat opportunities for wild animals (by way of roofs that accommodate bats and nesting birds, for instance, as exemplified by the traditional habits of storks and swallows in Europe).

However, the urban opportunities for non-human life can also be enhanced by our finding new ways for animals to 'earn their living' in the city. How might some of these new ways be envisaged? The usefulness of sheep as lawnmowers has been appreciated by a church in my own local neighbourhood, and there is no reason why other urban landholders, including local councils, should not follow suit. Sheep have also been used for traffic calming in the Netherlands, and strategic use of horse-drawn vehicles – for tourist rides or milk deliveries, for instance – could serve a similar purpose. City farms afford educational opportunities for urban schoolchildren increasingly distanced from the realities of food production. The possibilities for reintegrating animals productively into urban life are as limitless as our imaginations.

However, the principal way in which animals can earn a living in the city is still surely via their companionate role. The exclusive reign of the dog and the cat in this connection needs to be challenged, and the adaptability of other species to the human hearth and home investigated. There is immense scope for the conservation of native species, even endangered ones, in such a program of domestication. Species such as the quoll, or native cat, and the grey-headed flying fox, are reputed to make affectionate and contented hearth companions, and the domestic potentialities of many smaller, endangered wallabies, such as quokkas and bettongs, are relatively unexplored. (The quokkas on Rottnest Island, offshore from Perth in Western Australia, have already adapted to the kind of semi-tame, dump-side existence which is, according to certain evolutionary theorists, the first step in a species' self-surrender to domestication.) Our reluctance, as 'animal lovers', to countenance confinement of wild animals, and the loss of autonomy that domestication entails, may need to be offset by the recognition that humanity is just another potential niche in the biosphere, one which many species have in the past successfully occupied of their own free will.

The green city of the future, then, would be a mixed community rich in habitat opportunities for a great diversity of animal species. This reintegration of animals into human life would also help to expand human imaginative and empathetic horizons, undermining anthropocentrism and reinforcing commitment to the protection of the non-human world.

At the same time, the multiple contacts with animals that it would afford would enhance the health and sanity of the human population.

To envisage the green city of the future as a mixed community in this way would of course involve considerable rethinking of current urban and environmental planning principles. Restrictions on the ownership of native animals would have to be revised, and new local council regulations allowing for the responsible keeping of a wide range of 'pets' would be required.

Housing would have to be designed with the needs of both wild and tame non-human occupants in mind. Such demands on design would not in themselves militate against the medium-density housing currently favoured by town planners, but they would require that urban consolidation be counterbalanced by large increases in communal green space. Public spaces would also have to be rendered more hospitable to animals, with protection from traffic, and areas designated and set aside for inter-species exercise (dogs would presumably have to be kept apart from quokkas and quolls, for instance!).

Urban planners who currently concentrate on high-density development for the sake of energy conservation and curtailment of urban sprawl forget that, in excluding non-human beings from the city and creating human ghettos, they are intensifying the anthropocentric mind-set of urban populations.

The green city is one which not only conserves energy and utilises existing infrastructure but also challenges the traditional conceptual division between humankind and nature, making itself a frontier of ecological possibility and opening its people to the degree of contact with non-human life required to awaken their ecological sensibilities.

A Responsive World: Personal Reflections

Living with animals may indeed, then, be important, for us and for them and for the natural environment. But there is something larger at stake here, something that is difficult to articulate. It has to do with a sense of completeness, a certain texture that somehow holds us and makes our existence cohere with the greater scheme of things. I felt this texture when the backyard hummed with the elemental presence of Pookie during that long summer of our initiation into…something larger, more demanding, more generous than the scheduled life of our modern civilisation.

The loss of this texture makes our contemporary animal-exclusive existence curiously thin, curiously unreal despite our epic impositions on reality. I don't think I can really explain this sense of completeness; it is probably graspable only through experience. So in the remainder of this reflection let me continue the autobiographical thread and try to communicate, through recounting a little more of my own experience, that feeling of completeness, of barely perceptible cohering…

I grew up surrounded by loving animals on what today would be described as a hobby farm, situated on the rural outskirts of Melbourne. These animals included dogs and cats, ducks, geese, hens, and, at one stage, a turkey. There were brief episodes with sheep and cows. The main focus of my entire childhood, however, was my ponies.

My first pony, and the horses that came after her, were my day-long playmates and confidants. It was to them that I recited my earliest poems, and to them that I ran when I was hurt or excited. They nuzzled me in the same soft, considerate way whatever the occasion. I chose their company not for want of family and friends, but for its own sake. The form of intimacy that grew up between us was qualitatively different from anything that could have developed between myself and human persons.

It was a kind of uncluttered closeness, or being-with, which existed despite the fact that our subjectivities were, in terms of content, mutually unknowable.

We took it for granted, on either side, that this unknowability did not matter, that our psyches could touch and pervade each other, without need for explanations or self-disclosures, such as those conveyable by language. These animals were, for me, 'primary others', in the psychoanalytic sense; they were not substitutes for, but additional to, significant humans, nor could humans substitute for them. My subjectivity – my sense of self and world – was constituted through my 'object relations' with these animals just as fundamentally as it was through my relations with primary human others.

Domestic animals were not the only non-human influences shaping my sense of self and world in those early days. There were also kindly ancient gum trees on our land – we knew they dated from before colonisation because they bore canoe scars in their trunks. And there was the creek, steeped in elemental mystery for me, yet at the same time busy and loquacious, swirling with news of other unknown yet connected places. These, together with my animal family, and the wild birds and snakes, all contributed to my sense of a world of communicative presences beyond the circle of human concerns.

Nor was my childhood home the only place which turned my psyche outward in this way. There was also an old sheep station on the vast western plains of New South Wales, which I occasionally visited in school holidays. It was no ordinary sheep station but, even in those days, a relic of an earlier era. The owner, an old-timer with eyes as wide as the blue desert sky, had been born in the homestead and raised on the property, and he ran the place in the pre-mechanical style, with the aid of stock ponies, dogs and horse-drawn buggies.

We children were out all day in the searing sun on the saltbush plains, lunching out of battered tucker boxes, racing our ponies, chasing kangaroos, emus and wild pigs with delirious excitement. Back at the homestead, animals filled our every waking moment: there were sheep and lambs, of course, as well as the ponies, most of whom spent the main part of the year in a large herd out on the range, only coming in for a tour of duty now and again, as the need arose. (These tough but happy little horses lived to extraordinary ages. One died many years later at the age of forty-five!)

Cattle, pigs, tribes of chooks, ducks and geese, a flock of diminutive long-haired bush goats, an army of dogs, and at different times tame emus and kangaroos all congregated around the homestead. An old white goat named Snowy and a cocoa-coloured hand-reared filly clattered about on the wide back veranda. A sack containing a recently orphaned joey usually hung from the clothes line over the enormous wood-fired stove in the kitchen.

Compassion and fondness for animals jostled, in the daily round, with unabashed slaughter and brutality. From my saddle, I witnessed mother kangaroos being torn to shreds by dogs, 'for fun'; emus, in flight from our young stockman friends, failing to clear a fence, becoming entangled in the wire instead, and being bludgeoned to death with a fence post; and back at the homestead, pigs uttering torture-chamber screams as their throats were cut and their still-convulsing bodies dropped into troughs of scalding water.

I sat with the other kids in the back of a jeep on a kangaroo-shooting excursion and, as the bodies piled up under our feet, I remember the blood of the kangaroos soaking my green felt boots dark red. The cruelty shocked me to the core – in fact, it was this which first made me aware of my core, a still, silent, inner place of watching, beyond speech. But it did not diminish the overwhelming sense of enchantment that this place awakened in me. (Much, much later, I was to discover that the old station had had a similar effect on many of the people who had been associated with it.) For the enchantment, and the heightened feeling of being alive that accompanied it, arose from the fact that animals – and the uncompromising land which decided their fate – were the almost exclusive focus of everyone's life there, and the carnage, for all its horror, was part of that involvement.

When I was fifteen, my family moved into the inner city, and both my rural life, and my visits to the sheep station, ceased. However our new home overlooked extensive park lands, and I set up house with a dog in an old Victorian loft in our backyard, so the transition was not unduly traumatic. It was not until I was eighteen, when I abandoned my home and my country to live in London, that a keen sense of loss and deprivation at last set in. I moved in with a friend who leased a top-storey studio in the Kings Road in Chelsea, and for various reasons I was soon trapped in the life I had reluctantly chosen to lead there.

The apartment was without a garden, without the slightest glimpse of green from its high windows. The grand old building in which it was located was legendary as one of the nerve centres of the London 'underground'. Artists, writers and rock musicians congregated there, and every night, till dawn, the entire building was shaken with musical reverberations from the nightclub in the basement. People were embarked on what were for them exciting adventures with sex and drugs. The joint was unquestionably jumping. With comings and goings at all hours, residents and visitors alike were charged to the eyeballs with the fizz of glamour, the intoxication of notoriety and celebrity.

I alone, it seemed, languished. I felt deadened. Without any trees in sight, with all presence and memory of animals expunged from that world, without even a proper sky above me (the London sky appearing more like a low ceiling than the soaring invitation to infinity to which I was accustomed in Australia), I felt truly underground, buried alive.

My spirit, with its lifelong habit of expansiveness, had to submit for the first time to grey urban confinement, to a world built exclusively to human specifications, in which no court of appeal existed beyond socially prescribed perceptions and perspectives. There was here no turning out to a wider world of subtle voices and signals, a world of myriad, at first indiscernible, but with patient attention increasingly differentiated, responsive presences.

Rather, there was a turning in, and a turning up of the volume of human-generated and human-directed self-infatuated cacophony and chatter. This turning-in found its ultimate expression in the essential project of the counter-culture: to transform reality into an inner picture show, a spectacle of hallucinatory images and sexually induced sensations orchestrated for our private entertainment. This project was, in fact, nothing more than a hip rendition of the old transcendental idealism, or solipsistic anthropocentrism, of the Western tradition, which places reality in us rather than us in reality.

I had no words, at the time, to name this human introjection of reality, or to justify my sense of exile from a world that was truly alive, and, unlike the one in which I found myself, a source of true enlivenment. I especially had no words to challenge the high claims of Art on which the counter-culture rested. Instead, I kept some snails and bare twigs in a jar in my room, and gazed at them for months.

I retreated into a state of fantasy and intense creativity, writing and drawing obsessively, calling up from my own deep unconscious the images and motifs I needed to survive. I composed song cycles, and stories of origins, before I had heard of Aboriginal dreamings. I hung around old bookshops and antique stores, seeking out illustrations and folk tales that could be threaded into my nascent mythologies. I haunted the Natural History Museum in South Kensington, with its layer upon layer, colonnade after colonnade, of magical animal statuary. Whenever I found a numinous image – an old French engraving of a lone seal, for instance, or a Chinese painting of wild geese – I enshrined it, hanging it as a religious icon in the gallery of my mind. Out of such gathered fragments, and out of my own memory, imagination and dreams, I tried to recreate the sense of enchantment that had always been the essence of my experience of the world, and without which I did indeed find life scarcely worth living.

From the viewpoint of Western psychoanalysis, this sense of enchantment is regressive, and signals a failure of individuation in infancy. But to adopt this point of view is, of course, to beg the metaphysical question. Looking back on my early years now, it seems more plausible to me to assume that the ample opportunities for close communion with animals that were available to me throughout my childhood had opened me to a larger world, a world astir with presence or presences that vastly exceeded the human. It was this direct contact with unknowable but pervasive presence which instilled in me a sense of the sacredness or enchantment of the world, and the potentiality for magic within it.

'Magic' was, in this context, just the possibility of the world's response – the possibility, indeed probability, that the world, when invoked in good faith, will respond, though not necessarily in the manner one anticipates or with the results for which one hopes. One should certainly not, in my view, rely on this world to fulfil requests or afford protection, but if one entreats it simply to reveal itself, to engage in an act of communication, then, in my experience, it will generally do so, though in its own ever-unpredictable way.

I learned this as a child, through the receptiveness that my animal familiars created in me, and it filled my whole being with a sense of being accompanied, of never being alone, a sense of background love, akin to the background radiation of which physicists speak. This is a love which has nothing to do with saving us from death and suffering, or with making us happy.

From the viewpoint of the world, death and suffering are just inevitable concomitants of individual life. The point for individuals, from this perspective, is not to seek to evade these inevitabilities, but to reach beyond them – to call into the silence beyond human selfhood in search of a reply. This is the moment for which the world has been waiting, and in which it will rejoice: the moment when we ask it to speak.

To receive its reply is to enter a love far greater than the kind of protection and indulgence that our traditional importunate forms of prayer expect, for that reply signifies that we belong to an animate order, a pattern of meaning, from which death cannot separate us, and to which suffering only summons us.

To engage with the unknowable subjectivities of animals and to experience their response to us, particularly in childhood, is perhaps then a principal bridge to communication with the unknowable subjectivity of the wider world. To experience the world thus, as an inspirited thing, will not only direct the course of our own self-realisation in a most fundamental way; it will also ensure an attitude of profound mutuality and awed protectiveness towards the world itself.

Pookie RIP

It was only about three weeks after I had finished writing the story of Pookie that I had a phone call from Peter at Bindara farm. Pookie was dead. She had died in her sleep the previous night, Peter said, apparently from a heart attack. There was no sign of a struggle in the little pig house she shared with Wilber and she had appeared perfectly normal, and as cheeky as ever, when Peter had last seen her, at bedtime. She was eight years old, which is only middle-aged for a pig, but since there was possibly no tubbier pig on earth, the heart attack hypothesis was extremely plausible.

I was saddened by the news. It was hard to imagine the world without the feisty Pookster in it. But I was also disturbed. Why this strange conjunction between the writing of the story and the ending of the life? By finishing her story – which I had begun more than five years earlier – had I, by the mysterious and dangerous magic of writing, finished Pookie herself?

I know there are powerful taboos around what can be written, but I hadn't thought they would apply to Pookie – belching, farting, no-nonsense material girl that she was. But of course those taboos have nothing to do with old Christian contrasts between materiality and immateriality. On the other hand, however, this was a perfect death, taking Pookie without even waking her, in the midst of her supremely gratified life. Was there really any indication of the untoward in this?

As I pondered these questions, a vanished story from my very early childhood came to me. The story was called *The Cat Who Went To Heaven*, and it was a favourite of ours, famous for always making all of us, including mummy and daddy, cry. It told of a poor artist living long ago in a Japanese village. I am telling the story here as I found it, deep on the floor of memory's ocean, worn and whiskered and adulterated by self and time. I prefer to tell it this way rather than correcting it against the original.

With the last of his money, the artist sent his servant out to buy food but the servant bought a little kitten instead and brought it home, to his master's despair. However, just when it seemed that starvation was imminent, the young man received an assignment to paint a huge picture for the imperial palace. The painting was to depict the Buddha welcoming all the creatures of earth to heaven.

For months lengthening into years, the artist laboured on the canvas, painstakingly detailing every creature in creation. Every day the kitten, grown into an affectionate and sweet-natured cat, kept her master company, lightening his labour and his loneliness. At each day's end, she would come around to the front of the canvas and inspect it carefully. The master knew she was waiting for the expected depiction of a cat, but he was under the strictest imperial orders not to include a cat in the sacred scene, as cats were banned from the Buddhist heaven on account of their cruelty.

Years passed. The Buddha, larger and more beautiful and luminous than any real-life figure, stretched out his hand to bless a multitude of sentient beings, all lovingly portrayed down to the finest detail of their whiskers, claws, feathers and scales. Every sentient being was there, except one. The painting was nearly complete. Each day, the master's cat still came to inspect the day's work…and each day she went away crestfallen.

The master loved his cat more than anything in the world. He feared that her heart would break. But if he included her in the picture, the painting would be seen as blasphemous. It would be destroyed, all his effort would be wasted and ruin would be his lot.

Finally the painting was finished. It was one of the most beautiful paintings ever to have been created in the empire. But at the last moment the master, unable to face his small companion's heartbreak, painted a likeness of her inconspicuously in the bottom right-hand corner of the picture.

When his cat made her inspection that evening, she was overjoyed. So overjoyed was she, in fact, that she lay down in front of the canvas and died, from pure happiness. The poor master went to bed that night having lost not only his painting and his livelihood, but his beloved companion.

When he awoke the next morning, however, he found that the figure of the Buddha had turned in the night and was now extending its hand in blessing not to the assembled multitude but directly to the small bowed figure in the right-hand corner of the canvas. The miracle became known throughout the empire, and the painting was accepted by the emperor and universally acclaimed.

I am not suggesting that Pookie died of happiness at being immortalised in my little story. She was someone who couldn't have cared a toss about matters immortal. But just as the artist, by including his beautiful cat in the painting, overcame prejudice and opened the gates of heaven to cats, so, by telling the story of an adorable pig, one might make at least a tiny dent in the monumental prejudice that keeps millions of Pookies worldwide in unspeakable subjection and abjection.

If telling the tale of Pookie could achieve this, then her death, in the midst of pure happiness, might indeed begin to open a gate for other pigs, if not into heaven, then at least out of hell. May it be so.

Panel 1: my involvement with pigs started by chance. my mother was given a piglet for her birthday.

"let's call her pookie"

Panel 2: the breeder assured us that pookie was a miniature pig

"She'll grow no more than thirty kilos"

Panel 3: for the first few months she roamed our small brunswick backyard, jumping into my lap and tucking her head under my arm at every opportunity

Panel 4: but as she grew bigger she began to dislodge the paving and uproot the trees... gradually the yard was turning into one big wallow.

Panel 5: when she passed the 60 kg mark i built a sty for her at the back of the garden

Panel 6: though the sty was small she was quite content. it was the simple things that made her happy.

Panel 7: she had a blinding love of food... devouring bowls of weetbix, whole watermelons and boxes of rotten mangoes in an instant

Panel 8: second only to her love of food was her love of affection. she would always greet you with warm grunts and, rolling over, would invite you to rub her tummy

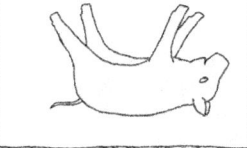

Panel 9: Sometimes i would sit with her for half an hour and talk to her. she could understand what i was saying – the sentiment if not the words.

Panel 10: befriending pookie meant that i started to become conscious of, and curious about, the existence of pigs in our world

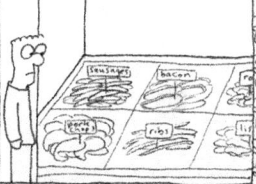

Panel 11: one day i rang up the bureau of statistics

"excuse me...um...how many pigs are there in victoria?"

"errr...let's see...hmm...3½ million are slaughtered annually"

Panel 12: three and a half million!!

Lightning Source UK Ltd.
Milton Keynes UK
UKOW05f2013030217

293569UK00022B/386/P

9 781760 410926